PRIMARY MATHEMATICS Standards Edition

TEXTBOOK

Marshall Cavendish Education

SingaporeMath.com Inc

Blank

Original edition published under the title Primary Mathematics Textbook 2A
© 1981 Curriculum Planning & Development Division, Ministry of Education, Singapore
Published by Times Media Private Limited

This edition © 2008 Marshall Cavendish International (Singapore) Private Limited

Published by Marshall Cavendish Education
An imprint of Marshall Cavendish
Marshall Cavendish is a trademark of Times Publishing Limited

Marshall Cavendish Corporation
99 White Plains Road
Tarrytown, NY 10591
U.S.A.
Tel: (1-914) 332 8888
Fax: (1-914) 332 8882
E-mail: mcc@marshallcavendish.com
Website: www.marshallcavendish.com

Distributed by
SingaporeMath.com Inc
404 Beavercreek Road #225
Oregon City, OR 97045
U.S.A.
Website: www.singaporemath.com

Marshall Cavendish International (Singapore) Private Limited
Times Centre, 1 New Industrial Road
Singapore 536196
Tel: +65 6411 0820
Fax: +65 6266 3677
E-mail: fps@sg.marshallcavendish.com
Website: www.marshallcavendish.com/education/sg

First published 2008
Reprinted 2008

Primary Mathematics (Standards Edition) Textbook 2A
ISBN 978-0-7614-6977-3

Printed in Singapore

Primary Mathematics (Standards Edition) is adapted from Primary Mathematics Textbook 2A (3rd Edition), originally
developed by the Ministry of Education, Singapore. This edition contains new content developed by Marshall Cavendish
International (Singapore) Private Limited, which is not attributable to the Ministry of Education, Singapore.

We would like to acknowledge the Project Team from the Ministry of Education, Singapore, that developed the original
Singapore Edition:
Project Director: Dr Kho Tek Hong
Team Members: Hector Chee Kum Hoong, Liang Hin Hoon, Lim Eng Tann,
        Ng Siew Lee, Rosalind Lim Hui Cheng, Ng Hwee Wan, Thong Chee Hing

Our thanks to Richard Askey, Emeritus Professor of Mathematics (University of Wisconsin, Madison) and Madge Goldman,
President (Gabriella and Paul Rosenbaum Foundation), for their help and advice in the production of Primary Mathematics
(Standards Edition).

We would also like to recognize the contribution of Jennifer Hoerst (Curriculum Advisor, SingaporeMath.com Inc) to Primary
Mathematics (Standards Edition).

PREFACE

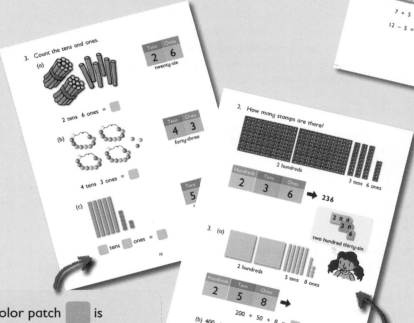

PRIMARY MATHEMATICS (Standards Edition) is a complete program from the publishers of Singapore's successful *Primary Mathematics* series. Newly adapted to align with the Mathematics Framework for California Public Schools, the program aims to equip students with sound concept development, critical thinking and efficient problem-solving skills.

Mathematical concepts are introduced in the opening pages and taught to mastery through specific learning tasks that allow for immediate assessment and consolidation.

The color patch ▮ is used to invite active student participation and to facilitate lively discussion about the mathematical concepts taught.

The **Concrete → Pictorial → Abstract** approach enables students to encounter math in a meaningful way and translate mathematical skills from the concrete to the abstract.

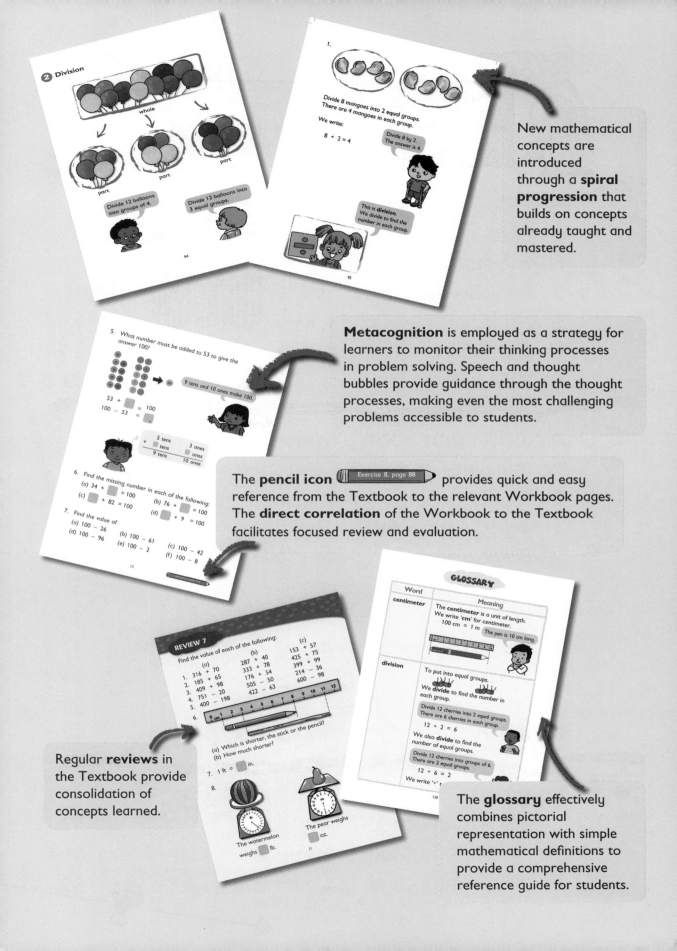

2 Division

whole

part

part

part

Divide 12 balloons into groups of 4.

Divide 12 balloons into 3 equal groups.

94

1.

Divide 8 mangoes into 2 equal groups.
There are 4 mangoes in each group.

We write:

$8 \div 2 = 4$

Divide 8 by 2.
The answer is 4.

This is **division**.
We divide to find the
number in each group.

95

New mathematical concepts are introduced through a **spiral progression** that builds on concepts already taught and mastered.

5. What number must be added to 53 to give the answer 100?

9 tens and 10 ones make 100.

$53 + \boxed{} = 100$
$100 - 53 = \boxed{}$

	5 tens	3 ones
+	☐ tens	☐ ones
	9 tens	10 ones

6. Find the missing number in each of the following:
   (a) $34 + \boxed{} = 100$
   (b) $76 + \boxed{} = 100$
   (c) $\boxed{} + 82 = 100$
   (d) $\boxed{} + 9 = 100$

7. Find the value of
   (a) $100 - 26$
   (b) $100 - 61$
   (c) $100 - 42$
   (d) $100 - 96$
   (e) $100 - 2$
   (f) $100 - 8$

12

Metacognition is employed as a strategy for learners to monitor their thinking processes in problem solving. Speech and thought bubbles provide guidance through the thought processes, making even the most challenging problems accessible to students.

The **pencil icon** Exercise 8, page 88 provides quick and easy reference from the Textbook to the relevant Workbook pages. The **direct correlation** of the Workbook to the Textbook facilitates focused review and evaluation.

REVIEW 7

Find the value of each of the following:

	(a)	(b)	(c)
1.	$316 + 70$	$287 + 40$	$153 + 57$
2.	$185 + 65$	$333 + 78$	$425 + 75$
3.	$409 + 98$	$176 + 54$	$399 + 99$
4.	$751 - 20$	$505 - 50$	$214 - 36$
5.	$400 - 198$	$422 - 63$	$600 - 98$

6.

0 cm 1 2 3 4 5 6 7 8 9 10 11 12

(a) Which is shorter, the stick or the pencil?
(b) How much shorter?

7. 1 ft = ☐ in.

8.

The watermelon weighs ☐ lb.

The pear weighs ☐ oz.

21

Regular **reviews** in the Textbook provide consolidation of concepts learned.

GLOSSARY

Word	Meaning
centimeter	The **centimeter** is a unit of length. We write 'cm' for centimeter. 100 cm = 1 m. The pen is 10 cm long.
division	To put into equal groups. We **divide** to find the number in each group. Divide 12 cherries into 2 equal groups. There are 6 cherries in each group. $12 \div 2 = 6$. We also **divide** to find the number of equal groups. Divide 12 cherries into groups of 6. There are 2 equal groups. $12 \div 6 = 2$. We write '÷' t...

128

The **glossary** effectively combines pictorial representation with simple mathematical definitions to provide a comprehensive reference guide for students.

CONTENTS

1 **Numbers to 1000**
1 Looking Back — 8
2 Hundreds, Tens and Ones — 13
3 Comparing Numbers — 20
REVIEW 1 — **23**

2 **Addition and Subtraction**
1 Meanings of Addition and Subtraction — 24
2 Addition Without Renaming — 32
3 Subtraction Without Renaming — 35
Practice A — 38
4 Addition with Renaming — 39
Practice B — 46
5 Subtraction with Renaming — 47
Practice C — 55
Practice D — 56
REVIEW 2 — **57**

3 **Length**
1 Measuring Length — 59
2 Measuring Length in Meters — 61
3 Measuring Length in Centimeters — 65

4   Measuring Length in Yards and Feet   70
5   Measuring Length in Inches   72
REVIEW 3   **74**

4   **Weight**
1   Measuring Weight in Kilograms   76
2   Measuring Weight in Grams   81
3   Measuring Weight in Pounds and Ounces   84
REVIEW 4   **88**

5   **Multiplication and Division**
1   Multiplication   90
   Practice A   93
2   Division   94
   Practice B   100
REVIEW 5   **101**

6   **Multiplication Tables of 2 and 3**
1   Multiplication Table of 2   104
2   Multiplication Table of 3   110
   Practice A   115
3   Dividing by 2   116
   Practice B   120
4   Dividing by 3   121
   Practice C   123
   Practice D   124
REVIEW 6   **125**

Glossary   **128**

Index   **135**

1 NUMBERS TO 1000

1 Looking Back

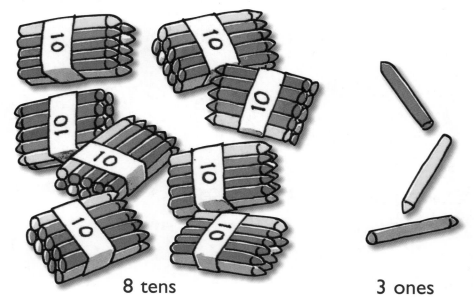

8 tens

3 ones

How many crayons are there altogether?

8 0   3 → 8 3

eighty-three

80 and 3 make 83.

8

1. (a) How many mangoes are there?

(b) 40 and 5 make ☐ .

(c) 5 more than 40 is ☐ .

(d) 40 + 5 = ☐

2. How many stamps are there?

Count by tens:
10, 20, 30, 40, 50,
60, 70, 80, 90, 100

10 tens make 1 hundred.

Exercise 1, pages 7-9

3. Count the tens and ones.

(a)

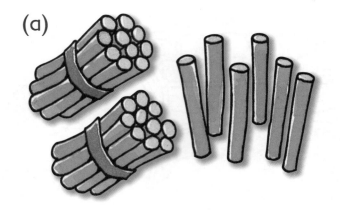

Tens	Ones
2	6

twenty-six

2 tens 6 ones =

(b)

Tens	Ones
4	3

forty-three

4 tens 3 ones =

(c)

Tens	Ones
5	7

fifty-seven

⬜ tens ⬜ ones = ⬜

4. Write the numbers in tens and ones.
   (a) 65   (b) 40   (c) 78   (d) 97

5. (a) What number is 4 more than 50?
   (b) What number is 3 more than 70?

6. Write the numbers in words.
   (a) 40   (b) 15   (c) 95   (d) 87

7. Write the numbers.
   (a) sixty-six   (b) eighty-one
   (c) 5 tens 3 ones   (d) 7 tens

Exercise 2, pages 10-11

8. This is a number chart from 1 to 100.
   Use it to do the following.

1	2	3	4	5	6	7	8	9	10
11	12	13	14	15	16	17	18	19	20
21	22	23	24	25	26	27	28	29	30
31	32	33	34	35	36	37	38	39	40
41	42	43	44	45	46	47	48	49	50
51	52	53	54	55	56	57	58	59	60
61	62	63	64	65	66	67	68	69	70
71	72	73	74	75	76	77	78	79	80
81	82	83	84	85	86	87	88	89	90
91	92	93	94	95	96	97	98	99	100

Arrange the numbers below in order.
Begin with the smallest.

76   87   78   67

9.

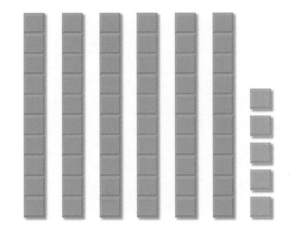

Tens	Ones
6	5

sixty-five

5 more than 60 is 65.

(a) What number is 1 more than 65?

(b) What number is 1 less than 65?

(c) What number is 10 more than 65?

(d) What number is 10 less than 65?

10. (a) What number is 2 more than 65?

(b) What number is 2 less than 65?

(c) What number is 20 more than 65?

(d) What number is 20 less than 65?

11. (a) 85 + 1 = ☐   (b) 85 + 2 = ☐

(c) 82 + 5 = ☐   (d) 82 + 20 = ☐

(e) 85 − 1 = ☐   (f) 85 − 2 = ☐

(g) 82 − 5 = ☐   (h) 82 − 20 = ☐

Exercise 3, pages 12-14

② Hundreds, Tens and Ones

I bundle the straws in tens. Then I put 10 tens together to make a hundred.

Count by hundreds.

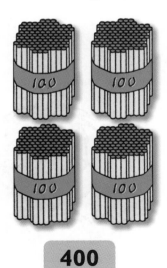

400

four hundred

100, 200, 300, 400

Count the straws.

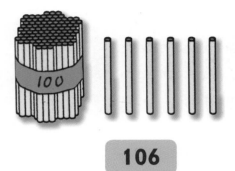

100, 101, 102, 103, 104, 105, 106

106

one hundred six

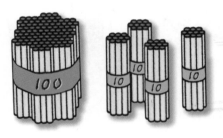

100, 110, 120, 130, 140

140

one hundred forty

100, 200, 210, 220, 221, 222, 223

223

two hundred twenty-three

100, 200, 300, 400, 500, 600, 700, 800, 900, 1000

10 hundreds make 1 thousand.

1000

one thousand

1. (a)

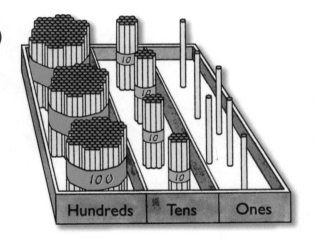

| Hundreds | Tens | Ones |

3 0 0
4 0
6

three hundred forty-six

3 hundreds 4 tens 6 ones = ☐

(b)

 hundreds tens ones =

15

Exercise 4, pages 15-16

2. How many stamps are there?

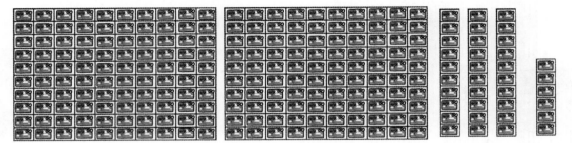

2 hundreds   3 tens   6 ones

Hundreds	Tens	Ones
2	3	6

➡ **236**

two hundred thirty-six

3. (a)

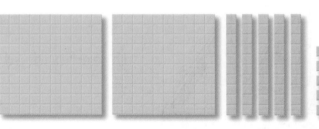

2 hundreds   5 tens   8 ones

Hundreds	Tens	Ones
2	5	8

➡

200 + 50 + 8 = ⬚

(b) 400 + 70 = ⬚   (c) 800 + 9 = ⬚

Exercise 5, pages 17-21

4. This is a one-hundred-dollar bill.

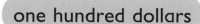 one hundred dollars

(a)

$460

four hundred sixty dollars

(b)

$604

six hundred four dollars

(c) How many ten-dollar bills can we change for a one-hundred-dollar bill?

5. This is a one-thousand-dollar bill.

one thousand dollars

How many one-hundred-dollar bills can we change for a one-thousand-dollar bill?

6. 10 = 1 1 1 1 1
        1 1 1 1 1

100 = 10 10 10 10 10
      10 10 10 10 10

1000 = 100 100 100 100 100
       100 100 100 100 100

(a) How many 1 can we change for a 100 ?

(b) How many 1 can we change for a 1000 ?

7. This chart shows 623.

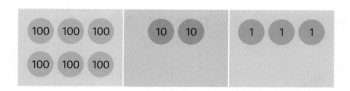

623 = ⬜ hundreds ⬜ tens ⬜ ones

8. What number does each chart show?

(a)

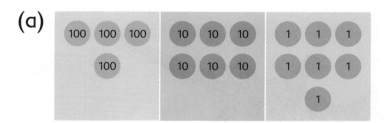

(b)

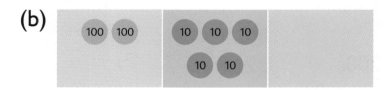

(c)

Exercise 6, pages 22-23

3 Comparing Numbers

210 is greater than 120.

We write: **210 > 120**

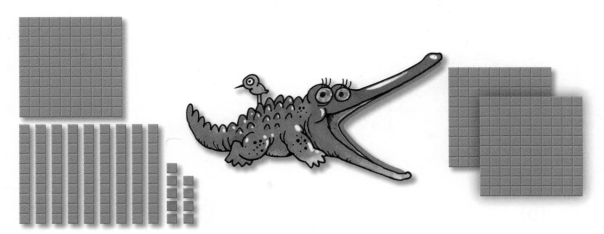

199 is less than 200.

We write: **199 < 200**

1. Which sign should you use, **>** or **<**?

(a)

   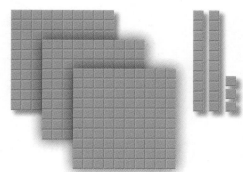

232 ◯ 323

(b)

Hundreds	Tens	Ones
9	5	0

Hundreds	Tens	Ones
7	6	4

950 ◯ 764

(c) 361 ◯ 438   (d) 429 ◯ 439

(e) 847 ◯ 841   (f) 97 ◯ 201

(g) 600 + 40 ◯ 604   (h) 900 + 9 ◯ 990

2. (a) Which number is smaller, 412 or 398?
   (b) Which number is greater, 62 or 520?
   (c) Which number is the smallest: 540, 405 or 425?
   (d) What is the smallest number that can be made using the digits 6, 4 and 3?

3. Arrange the numbers in order.
   Begin with the smallest.

   364 436 463 346

21

Exercise 7, pages 24-25

4. (a) What number is 1 more than 253?

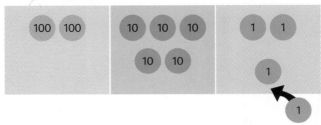

(b) What number is 10 more than 123?

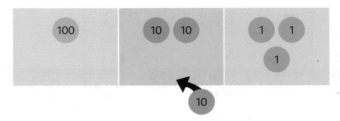

(c) What number is 100 less than 341?

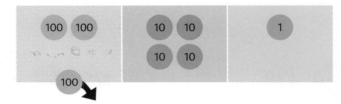

5. (a) Count on in steps of 1.
   345, 346, 347, ... 351

   (b) Count on in steps of 10.
   475, 485, 495, ... 535

   (c) Count on in steps of 100.
   105, 205, 305, ... 705

   (d) Count backwards in steps of 10.
   840, 830, 820, ... 780

6. Complete these regular number patterns.

   (a) 197, 198, 199, ▢   (b) 308, ▢ , 328, 338, 348

   (c) 932, 832, 732, ▢ , 532   (d) 722, 712, 702, ▢

22

Exercise 8, pages 26-27

1. Write the numbers in words.
   (a) 330   (b) 144   (c) 255   (d) 608

2. Write the numbers in hundreds, tens and ones.
   (a) 645   (b) 720   (c) 409   (d) 900

3. Write the numbers.
   (a) seven hundred four
   (b) five hundred forty
   (c) 3 hundreds 4 ones
   (d) 8 hundreds 2 tens

4. Which sign should you use, > or <?
   (a) 439 ⬤ 426   (b) 290 ⬤ 300
   (c) 506 ⬤ 56   (d) 620 ⬤ 602

5. Arrange the numbers in order.
   Begin with the smallest.
   (a) 99, 609, 410
   (b) 410, 140, 401, 104

6. (a) What number is 1 more than 299?
   (b) What number is 1 less than 780?

7. (a) What number is 10 more than 462?
   (b) What number is 10 less than 800?

8. (a) What number is 100 more than 599?
   (b) What number is 100 less than 605?

Review 1, pages 28-30

ADDITION AND SUBTRACTION

1 **Meanings of Addition and Subtraction**

Ali has **8** toy cars.
David has **6** toy cars.
How many toy cars do they have altogether?

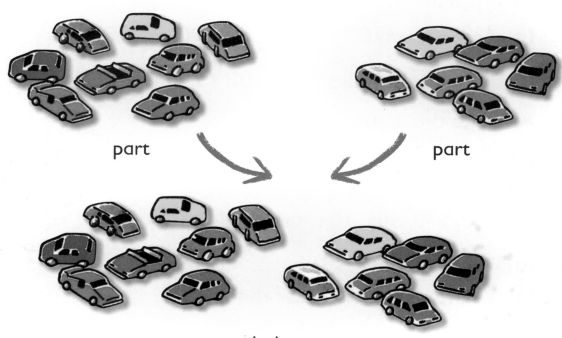

part   part

whole

8 + 6 =

They have   toy cars altogether.

24

Ali and David have **14** toy cars altogether.
Ali has **8** toy cars.
How many toy cars does David have?

14 − 8 =

To find the whole, we add.
To find one part, we subtract.

David has ☐ toy cars.

1.

7 + 5 = ☐   5 + 7 = ☐

12 − 5 = ☐   12 − 7 = ☐

2.

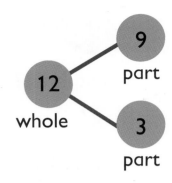

9 + 3 = [ ]   3 + 9 = [ ]

12 − 3 = [ ]   12 − 9 = [ ]

3. Mr. Stone bought 7 chicken burritos
and 8 beef burritos.
How many burritos did he buy?

He bought [ ] burritos.

4. Haley had 16 stamps.
She gave 9 of them away.
How many stamps did she have left?

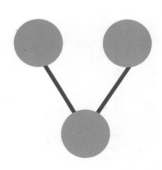

She had [ ] stamps left.

Exercise 1, page 31

5.

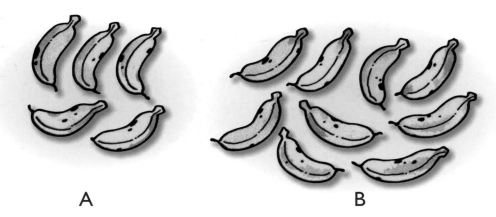

A　　　　　　　　　　　B

(a) How many more bananas are there in Set B than in Set A?

(b) 9 − 5 = ☐

6. (a) 14 − 8 = ☐

(b) 8 less than 14 is ☐.

7. There are 12 cherries and 5 pears.
   How many more cherries than pears are there?

   12 − 5 = ☐

   There are ☐ more cherries than pears.

8. Marisol wants to buy this book.
   She has only $9.
   How much more money does she need?

   $19 − $9 = $☐

   She needs $☐ more.

27

Exercise 2, pages 32-33

9. Add 21 and 35.

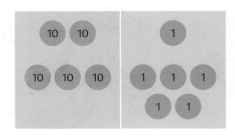

$$21 + 35 = \boxed{}$$

10. Subtract 13 from 27.

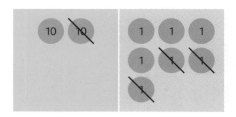

$$27 - 13 = \boxed{}$$

11.

$$32 + 13 = \boxed{} \qquad 13 + 32 = \boxed{}$$

$$45 - 13 = \boxed{} \qquad 45 - 32 = \boxed{}$$

12. Find the value of
    (a) 34 + 3
    (b) 97 + 2
    (c) 56 + 20
    (d) 61 + 27
    (e) 42 + 35
    (f) 58 + 40

13. Find the value of
    (a) 65 − 4
    (b) 79 − 40
    (c) 64 − 44
    (d) 86 − 35
    (e) 67 − 31
    (f) 45 − 23

 Exercise 3, pages 34-35

14. Danny has 34 key chains.
    He buys 5 more.
    How many key chains does he have now?

    34 + 5 = ☐

    Danny has ☐ key chains now.

15. There are 24 green apples and 32 red apples.
    How many apples are there altogether?

    24 + 32 = ☐

    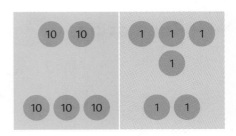

    There are ☐ apples altogether.

16. Michael had **78** goldfish.
    He sold **40** of them.
    How many goldfish did he have left?

$$78 - 40 = \boxed{}$$

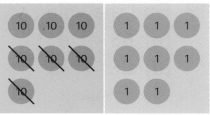

He had $\boxed{}$ goldfish left.

17. Rahmat has **48** stickers.
    Samy has **32** stickers.
    How many more stickers does Rahmat have than Samy?

$$48 - 32 = \boxed{}$$

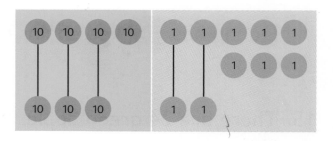

Rahmat has $\boxed{}$ more stickers than Samy.

18. Mr. Gray sold 23 drinks in the morning.
He sold 76 drinks in the afternoon.
How many drinks did he sell altogether?

23  76 =

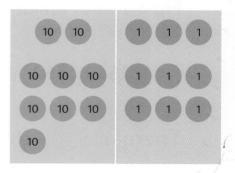

He sold ___ drinks altogether.

19. There are 58 cows and 23 horses on a farm.
How many fewer horses than cows are there?

58 ___ 23 =

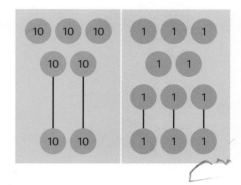

There are ___ fewer horses than cows.

Exercise 4, pages 36-37

② Addition Without Renaming

There are 236 boys and 362 girls.
How many children are there?

236 + 362 =

There are ⬜ children.

We can add like this:

```
  H T O
  2 3 6
+ 3 6 2
-------
  5 9 8
```

100 100
100 100 100

10 10 10
10 10 10
10 10 10

1 1 1
1 1 1
1 1

Add the ones.
6 ones + 2 ones
= **8** ones

Add the tens.
3 tens + 6 tens
= **9** tens

Add the hundreds.
2 hundreds + 3 hundreds
= **5** hundreds

Add the ones.
```
  2 3 6
+ 3 6 2
-------
      8
```

Add the tens.
```
  2 3 6
+ 3 6 2
-------
    9 8
```

Add the
hundreds.
```
  2 3 6
+ 3 6 2
-------
  5 9 8
```

32

1. (a) 2 + 3 =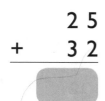

   (b) 20 + 30 =

   (c) 200 + 300 =

2. Add 25 and 32.

$$\begin{array}{r} 2\,5 \\ +\quad 3\,2 \\ \hline \end{array}$$

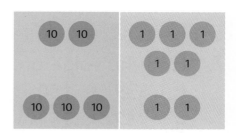

3. Find the value of
   (a) 61 + 8   (b) 75 + 4   (c) 34 + 24
   (d) 19 + 50   (e) 60 + 34   (f) 70 + 29

4. Add 251 and 34.

$$\begin{array}{r} 2\,5\,1 \\ +\quad 3\,4 \\ \hline \end{array}$$

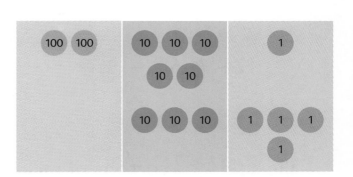

5. Find the value of
   (a) 104 + 30   (b) 230 + 60   (c) 125 + 72
   (d) 539 + 50   (e) 834 + 15   (f) 104 + 22

Exercise 5, pages 38-39

6. Add 245 and 142.

$$
\begin{array}{r}
2\ 4\ 5 \\
+\ \ 1\ 4\ 2 \\
\hline
\end{array}
$$

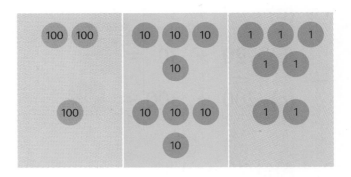

7. Find the value of
   (a) 539 + 150   (b) 442 + 134
   (c) 342 + 253   (d) 250 + 129
   (e) 125 + 742   (f) 305 + 202

8. Mr. Lin sold 124 cartons of milk on Saturday.
   He sold 65 cartons of milk on Sunday.
   How many cartons of milk did he sell altogether?

   124 + 65 = ☐

$$
\begin{array}{r}
1\ 2\ 4 \\
+\ \ \ \ 6\ 5 \\
\hline
\end{array}
$$

He sold ☐ cartons of milk altogether.

Exercise 6, pages 40-41

3 Subtraction Without Renaming

There are **396** children.
214 of them are boys.
How many girls are there?

396 − 214 =

There are ☐ girls.

We can subtract like this:

```
H T O
  3 9 6
−   2 1 4
─────────
  1 8 2
```

Subtract the
ones.
6 ones − 4 ones
= **2** ones

Subtract the tens.
9 tens − 1 ten
= **8** tens

Subtract the hundreds.
3 hundreds − 2 hundreds
= **1** hundred

Subtract the ones.
```
  3 9 6
−   2 1 4
─────────
      2
```

Subtract the tens.
```
  3 9 6
−   2 1 4
─────────
    8 2
```

Subtract the hundreds.
```
  3 9 6
−   2 1 4
─────────
  1 8 2
```

1. (a) $7 - 3 = $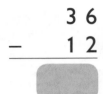

   (b) $70 - 30 = $

   (c) $700 - 300 = $

2. Subtract 12 from 36.

$$\begin{array}{r} 3\ 6 \\ -\ \ 1\ 2 \\ \hline \end{array}$$

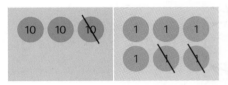

3. Find the value of
   (a) $78 - 4$ (b) $65 - 5$ (c) $78 - 40$
   (d) $65 - 50$ (e) $59 - 37$ (f) $48 - 38$

4. Subtract 25 from 239.

$$\begin{array}{r} 2\ 3\ 9 \\ -\ \ \ \ 2\ 5 \\ \hline \end{array}$$

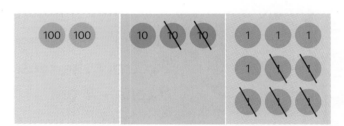

5. Find the value of
   (a) $486 - 80$ (b) $178 - 10$ (c) $597 - 85$
   (d) $269 - 62$ (e) $536 - 13$ (f) $648 - 22$

Exercise 7, pages 42-43

6. Subtract 152 from 376.

         3 7 6
       −   1 5 2
         [   ]

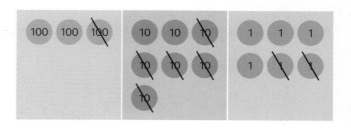

7. Find the value of
    (a) 321 − 100   (b) 682 − 140
    (c) 938 − 416   (d) 872 − 761
    (e) 365 − 145   (f) 486 − 160

8. There were 287 people in a hall.
    52 of them were children.
    How many adults were there?

         2 8 7
       −   5 2
         [   ]

    287 − 52 = [   ]

    There were [   ] adults.

37

Exercise 8, pages 44-45

PRACTICE A

Find the value of each of the following:

	(a)	(b)	(c)
1.	354 + 5	147 + 21	253 + 346
2.	865 − 3	694 − 72	484 − 43
3.	163 + 30	267 + 300	185 + 412
4.	588 − 60	794 − 500	385 − 161
5.	364 + 124	856 − 354	697 − 90

6. After selling 245 buns, Mrs. Bates was left with 54 buns. How many buns did she have at first?

7. In a class library, there are 568 English books and 204 Spanish books. How many more English books than Spanish books are there?

8. Maria had 439 eggs. She sold 326 of them. How many eggs did she have left?

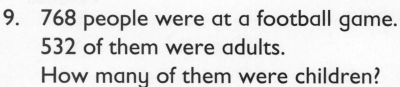
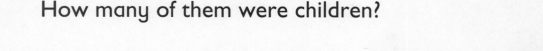

9. 768 people were at a football game. 532 of them were adults. How many of them were children?

10. 104 boys and 125 girls took part in a swimming test.
   (a) How many children took part in the test?
   (b) How many more girls than boys were there?

④ Addition with Renaming

Add 36 and 28.

```
   3 6
 + 2 8
```

When there are 10 ones
or more, change
10 ones for 1 ten.

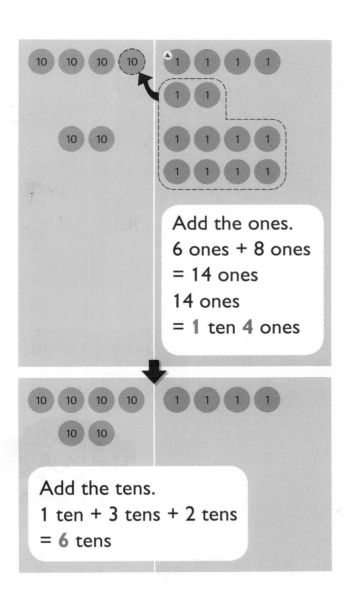

Add the ones.
6 ones + 8 ones
= 14 ones
14 ones
= **1** ten **4** ones

Add the tens.
1 ten + 3 tens + 2 tens
= **6** tens

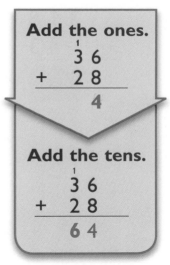

Add the ones.
```
   3 6
 + 2 8
─────────
       4
```

Add the tens.
```
   3 6
 + 2 8
─────────
     6 4
```

1. Find the value of
   (a) 4 + 9   (b) 60 + 9   (c) 64 + 9
   (d) 40 + 90   (e) 600 + 9   (f) 640 + 90

Exercise 9, page 46

2. Find the value of
   (a) 35 + 7   (b) 75 + 5   (c) 48 + 38
   (d) 54 + 29   (e) 57 + 13   (f) 69 + 31

3. Add 318 and 43.

```
    3 1 8
  +   4 3
```

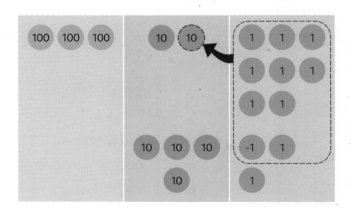

Change 10 ones for 1 ten.

4. Find the value of
   (a) 315 + 8   (b) 224 + 7   (c) 527 + 45
   (d) 608 + 48   (e) 734 + 36   (f) 321 + 69

5. Add 267 and 123.

$$\begin{array}{r} 2\ 6\ 7 \\ +\ \ 1\ 2\ 3 \\ \hline \end{array}$$

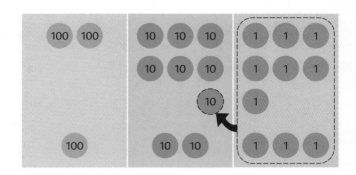

6. Find the value of
   (a) 127 + 365   (b) 452 + 219   (c) 639 + 124
   (d) 745 + 136   (e) 506 + 104   (f) 828 + 162

7. Lily is 18 years old.
   Her father is 26 years older than she.
   How old is her father?

   18 + 26 =

   Her father is   years old.

8. Diane saved $125.
   Seth saved $36 more than Diane.
   How much did Seth save?

   $125 + $36 = $

   Seth saved $.

41

Exercise 10, pages 47-48

9. Add 563 and 56.

$$
\begin{array}{r}
5\ 6\ 3 \\
+\quad\ 5\ 6 \\
\hline
\end{array}
$$

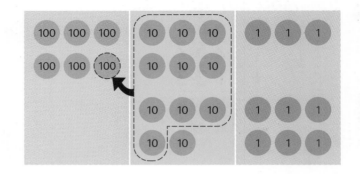

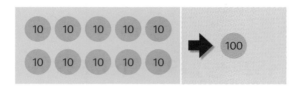

Change 10 tens for 1 hundred.

10. Find the value of
    (a) 292 + 60
    (b) 574 + 70
    (c) 385 + 63
    (d) 630 + 94
    (e) 420 + 80
    (f) 279 + 30

11. Add 382 and 145.

$$
\begin{array}{r}
3\ 8\ 2 \\
+\quad 1\ 4\ 5 \\
\hline
\end{array}
$$

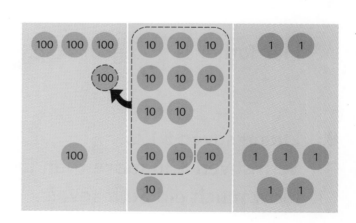

12. Find the value of
    (a) 454 + 163
    (b) 670 + 156
    (c) 257 + 351
    (d) 588 + 220
    (e) 363 + 255
    (f) 790 + 139

13. After selling **86** bags of popcorn, Mrs. Miguel had 22 bags of popcorn left.
How many bags of popcorn did she have at first?

86 + 22 = ▢

She had ▢ bags of popcorn at first.

14. A tailor bought **240** white buttons and **85** black buttons.
How many buttons did he buy altogether?

```
  2 4 0
+   8 5
───────
  ▢
```

He bought ▢ buttons.

Exercise 11, pages 49-51

15. Add **248** and **75**.

```
  2 4 8
+   7 5
───────
  ▢
```

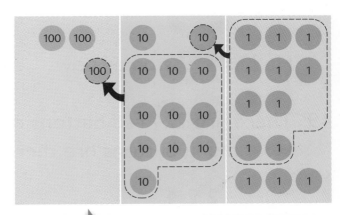

¹
2 4 8
+   7 5
─────
     3
	¹ ¹
	2 4 8
	+ 7 5
	─────
	  2 3
		¹ ¹
		2 4 8
		+ 7 5
		─────
		3 2 3

Add the ones.	**Add the tens.**	**Add the hundreds.**

16. Add 237 and 184.

$$\begin{array}{r} 2\ 3\ 7 \\ +\ \ 1\ 8\ 4 \\ \hline \end{array}$$

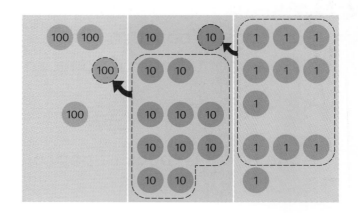

17. Find the value of
    (a) 265 + 69   (b) 493 + 28   (c) 684 + 19
    (d) 178 + 443   (e) 204 + 398   (f) 465 + 135

18. Carl has 169 stamps.
    His friend gives him 71 more.
    How many stamps does he have now?

$$\begin{array}{r} 1\ 6\ 9 \\ +\ \ \ \ 7\ 1 \\ \hline \end{array}$$

He has ☐ stamps now.

19. There are 224 red buttons and 298 yellow buttons.
    How many buttons are there altogether?

$$\begin{array}{r} 2\ 2\ 4 \\ +\ \ 2\ 9\ 8 \\ \hline \end{array}$$

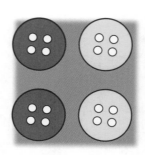

There are ☐ buttons altogether.

Exercise 12, pages 52-54

20. Add 186, 249 and 38.

```
    1 8 6
    2 4 9
+     3 8
```

We add 3 numbers in the same way.

```
  2
  1 8 6
  2 4 9
+   3 8
      3
```
Add the ones.

```
  1 2
  1 8 6
  2 4 9
+   3 8
    7 3
```
Add the tens.

```
  1 2
  1 8 6
  2 4 9
+   3 8
  4 7 3
```
Add the hundreds.

21. Find the value of
  (a) 172 + 487 + 74   (b) 209 + 145 + 567
  (c) 293 + 128 + 60   (d) 358 + 217 + 330

22. There were 102 boys, 86 girls and 40 adults at a concert.
    How many people were there at the concert?

```
    1 0 2
      8 6
+     4 0
```

There were ☐ people at the concert.

Exercise 13, pages 55-56

Find the value of each of the following:

	(a)	(b)	(c)
1.	26 + 9	32 + 8	46 + 7
2.	35 + 28	51 + 29	63 + 27
3.	27 + 80	33 + 82	49 + 70
4.	53 + 62	64 + 65	72 + 37
5.	44 + 56	58 + 42	74 + 26
6.	490 + 139	584 + 250	876 + 19
7.	407 + 38	532 + 48	644 + 49
8.	745 + 108	829 + 122	667 + 227
9.	264 + 50	379 + 60	342 + 93
10.	293 + 60 + 24	339 + 104 + 40	224 + 106 + 320

11. Mark scored 27 goals for his ice hockey team
    one season.
    Dylan scored 5 goals more than Mark.
    How many goals did Dylan score?

12. There are 427 cars in Parking Lot A.
    There are 278 cars in Parking Lot B.
    How many cars are there in the two parking lots?

13. Juan sold 46 cream puffs in the morning.
    He sold another 28 in the afternoon.
    He still had 16 cream puffs left.
    (a) How many cream puffs did he sell?
    (b) How many cream puffs did he have at first?

⑤ Subtraction with Renaming

Subtract 43 from 62.

```
  6 2
- 4 3
```

When there are not enough ones to subtract from, change 1 ten for 10 ones.

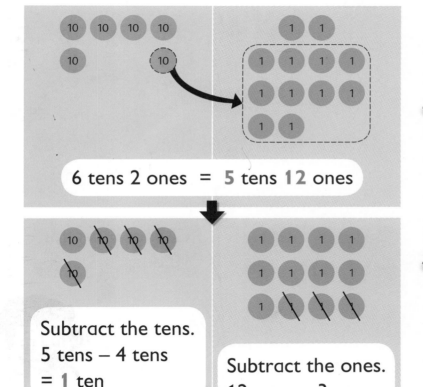

6 tens 2 ones = **5** tens **12** ones

Subtract the tens.
5 tens − 4 tens
= **1** ten

Subtract the ones.
12 ones − 3 ones
= **9** ones

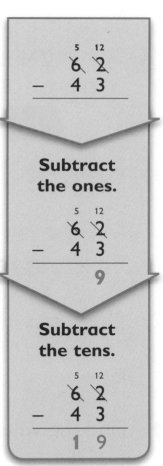

Subtract the ones.

Subtract the tens.

1. Find the value of
   (a) 10 – 6   (b) 11 – 6   (c) 41 – 6
   (d) 100 – 60   (e) 110 – 60   (f) 410 – 60

2. Find the value of
   (a) 30 – 6   (b) 41 – 9   (c) 52 – 13
   (d) 63 – 35   (e) 74 – 48   (f) 86 – 58

3. Subtract 18 from 243.

$$\begin{array}{r} 2\ 4\ 3 \\ -\ \ \ \ 1\ 8 \\ \hline \end{array}$$

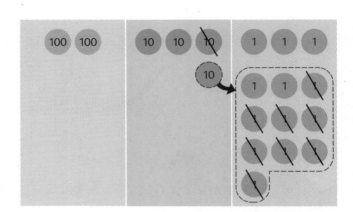

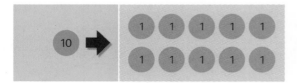

Change 1 ten for 10 ones.

4. Find the value of
   (a) 354 – 9   (b) 480 – 7   (c) 562 – 34
   (d) 690 – 45   (e) 720 – 18   (f) 833 – 29

5. Subtract 134 from 452.

$$\begin{array}{r} 4\ 5\ 2 \\ -\ \ 1\ 3\ 4 \\ \hline \end{array}$$

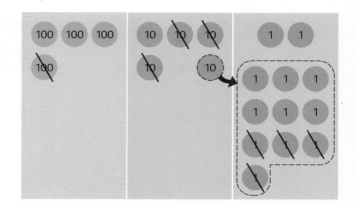

6. Find the value of
   (a) 441 − 227   (b) 553 − 228   (c) 764 − 506
   (d) 470 − 256   (e) 625 − 118   (f) 830 − 724

7. Mrs. Cohen went shopping with $92.
   She spent $58.
   How much money did she have left?

   $92 − $58 = $ ☐

   She had $ ☐ left.

8. There are 390 chairs in a hall.
   189 of them are new.
   How many chairs are **not** new?

   390 − 189 = ☐

   ☐ chairs are not new.

Exercise 14, pages 57-58

9. Subtract 64 from 729.

$$\begin{array}{r} 7\ 2\ 9 \\ -\ \ \ \ 6\ 4 \\ \hline \end{array}$$

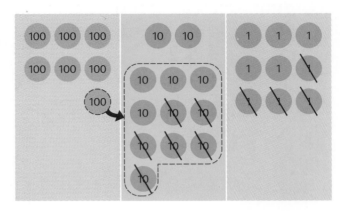

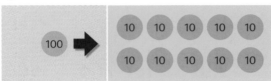

Change 1 hundred for 10 tens.

10. Find the value of
(a) 348 − 76   (b) 409 − 38   (c) 516 − 54
(d) 707 − 61   (e) 620 − 80   (f) 139 − 83

11. Subtract 293 from 538.

$$\begin{array}{r} 5\ 3\ 8 \\ -\ 2\ 9\ 3 \\ \hline \end{array}$$

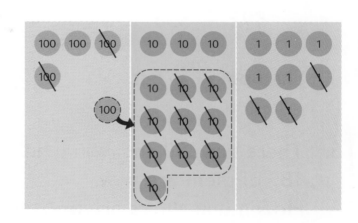

12. Find the value of
(a) 617 − 247   (b) 308 − 140   (c) 705 − 492
(d) 807 − 486   (e) 634 − 284   (f) 920 − 840

13. Jose bought 125 greeting cards.
    He used 42 of them.
    How many cards did he have left?

```
    1 2 5
  −   4 2
```
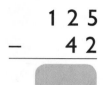

He had 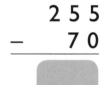 cards left.

14. Justin made 255 pizzas.
    He sold some of them and had 70 pizzas left.
    How many pizzas did he sell?

```
    2 5 5
  −   7 0
```

He sold ▮ pizzas.

15. Brian has 235 American stamps and 182 Canadian stamps.
    How many more American stamps than Canadian stamps
    does he have?

```
    2 3 5
  − 1 8 2
```

He has ▮ more American stamps than
Canadian stamps.

Exercise 15, pages 59-60

16. Subtract 68 from 421.

$$
\begin{array}{r}
4\ 2\ /1 \\
-\quad\ 6\ 8 \\
\hline
\end{array}
$$

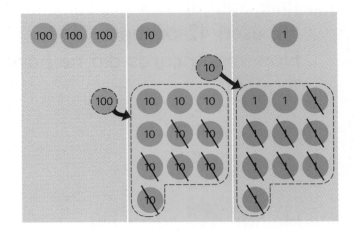

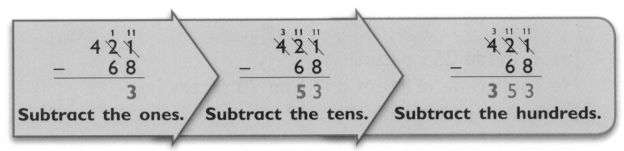

Subtract the ones.   Subtract the tens.   Subtract the hundreds.

17. Find the value of
    (a) 322 − 47   (b) 430 − 55   (c) 631 − 78

18. Subtract 267 from 453.

$$
\begin{array}{r}
4\ 5\ 3 \\
-\ 2\ 6\ 7 \\
\hline
\end{array}
$$

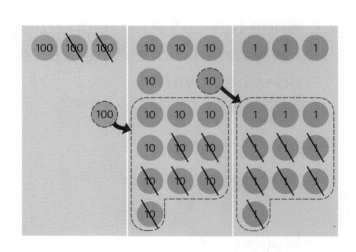

19. Find the value of
    (a) 512 − 149   (b) 640 − 276   (c) 623 − 246

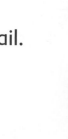

20. Jenny collected 120 shells.
    She collected 14 more shells than Abigail.
    How many shells did Abigail collect?

```
    1 2 0
  −   1 4
```
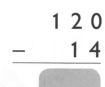

    Abigail collected shells.

21. Lydia needs 620 beads to make a bag.
    She has only 465 beads.
    How many more beads does she need?

```
    6 2 0
  − 4 6 5
```
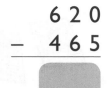

    She needs more beads.

Exercise 16, pages 61-62

22. Subtract 28 from 300.

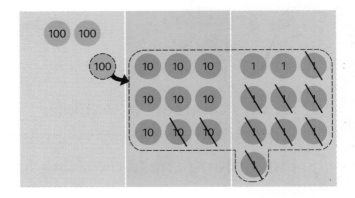

Change 1 hundred for 9 tens and 10 ones.

23. Find the value of
    (a) 400 − 38   (b) 700 − 276   (c) 402 − 337
    (d) 600 − 423   (e) 703 − 287   (f) 904 − 827

24. Seth had 105 picture cards.
    After giving some away, he had
    87 picture cards left.
    How many picture cards did he give away?

```
    1 0 5
  −   8 7
```

He gave away ▢ picture cards.

Exercise 17, pages 63-64

Find the value of each of the following:

	(a)	(b)	(c)
1.	40 – 8	50 – 12	60 – 24
2.	41 – 14	52 – 23	63 – 38
3.	53 – 35	64 – 16	74 – 29
4.	70 – 61	80 – 73	90 – 89
5.	73 – 68	82 – 77	91 – 86
6.	400 – 80	502 – 70	630 – 90
7.	100 – 23	400 – 92	503 – 78
8.	290 – 128	370 – 163	460 – 253
9.	530 – 139	642 – 248	753 – 359

10. Sara bought 84 T-shirts.
    She gave 15 of them to her friends.
    How many T-shirts did she have left?

11. Sally and Kelly have 98 postcards altogether.
    Sally has 39 postcards.
    How many postcards does Kelly have?

12. The total cost of a calculator and a watch is $212.
    The watch costs $144.
    (a) Find the cost of the calculator.
    (b) Which costs more, the watch
        or the calculator?
    (c) How much more?

Exercise 18, pages 65-66

Find the value of each of the following:

	(a)	(b)	(c)
1.	40 + 39	52 + 27	61 + 38
2.	79 − 20	82 − 42	96 − 90
3.	70 + 38	64 + 16	35 + 77
4.	261 − 52	473 − 60	560 − 246
5.	122 + 77	236 + 58	347 + 359

6. Anna has 18 storybooks.
   Kim has 14 more storybooks than Anna.
   How many storybooks does Kim have?

7. The table shows the result of a basketball game between two teams.

Team A	79 points
Team B	95 points

   (a) Which team scored more points?
   (b) How many more points did the winning team score?

8. 140 children took part in a swimming test.
   23 of them failed the test.
   How many children passed the test?

9. Angela had $220.
   After buying a watch, she had $186 left.
   How much did the watch cost?

Exercise 19, pages 67-68

REVIEW 2

	(a)	(b)	(c)
1.	80 − 47	71 − 36	92 − 87
2.	66 + 34	79 + 22	88 + 19
3.	350 − 49	408 − 148	607 − 560
4.	247 + 37	375 + 180	408 + 199
5.	500 − 142	603 − 266	710 − 614

6. Write the numbers.
   (a) Six hundred six
   (b) Eight hundred fifty-five
   (c) Four hundred forty

7. Write these numbers in words.
   (a) 250   (b) 744   (c) 307   (d) 922

8. Arrange these numbers in order.
   Begin with the smallest.

   928   930   909   912

9. Write >, < or = in place of each .

   (a) 370 + 40 ◯ 400

   (b) 132 + 40 ◯ 130 + 42

   (c) 139 + 600 ◯ 139 + 60

   (d) 259 + 60 ◯ 249 + 70

10. A farmer has **82** chickens.
    He has **24** more ducks than chickens.
    How many ducks does he have?

11. Holly bought this dictionary.
    She had **$28** left.
    How much money did she have at first?

12. There are **152** desks in a hall.
    There are **35** fewer chairs than desks.
    How many chairs are there in the hall?

13. David is **26** years old.
    Paul is **9** years older than David.
    Mary is **8** years older than Paul.
    (a) How old is Paul?
    (b) How old is Mary?

14. There are **304** girls in a school.
    There are **46** fewer boys than girls.
    (a) How many boys are there in the school?
    (b) How many children are there in the school?

15. There are **203** girls, **142** boys and **84** adults at a park.
    (a) How many people are at the park?
    (b) How many more girls than boys are at the park?

1 Measuring Length

How long is the bridge if we use Mother Duck's footprints to measure it?

How long is the bridge if we use Baby Duck's footprints to measure it?

1. Measure the length of your book with long paper clips.
   Measure the length of your book with short paper clips.
   (a) How many long paper clips did you use?
   (b) How many short paper clips did you use?
   (c) Which is greater, the number of long paper clips or
       the number of short paper clips?

2. Measure the width of your classroom door.

   The door is [ ] footprints wide.

3.

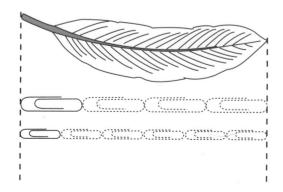

The feather is about

[ ] large paper clips long.

The feather is about

[ ] small paper clips long.

2 Measuring Length in Meters

1 meter

Jamal   Ben

Who is taller than 1 meter?
Who is shorter than 1 meter?

Measure your height with a meter rule.
Are you taller than 1 meter or shorter than 1 meter?

1. Measure your teacher's desk with a meter rule.

2. Cut a string 1 meter long.
Use it to measure the length of the whiteboard in your classroom.

Is the length of the whiteboard more than 3 m or less than 3 m?

3. Work in groups.
   Cut a string which you think is 1 m long.
   Check the length of the string with a meter rule.
   Is the string longer than 1 m or shorter than 1 m?

4. Use a meter rule or a string which is 1 m long.
   Check (✓) the correct box in the table.

	Less than 1 m	More than 1 m
My height		
My reach		
Length of my desk		
Width of my desk		
Height of my desk		

5. Use a meter rule or a string which is 1 m long.
   Estimate and then measure the following lengths.

	My estimate	My measure
Length of the whiteboard	about ___ m	about ___ m
Length of one side of the classroom	about ___ m	about ___ m

6.

7 m

4 m

The red ribbon is 7 m long.
The blue ribbon is 4 m long.
(a) What is the total length of the two ribbons?
(b) How much longer is the red ribbon than the blue ribbon?

7.

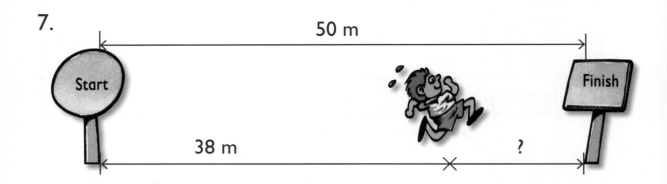

Paul is running in a 50-meter race.
He is 38 m from the starting point.
How many meters is he from the finishing point?

8. Mrs. Fernandez bought 60 m of cloth.
After making some curtains, she had 24 m of cloth left.
How many meters of cloth did she use?

3 Measuring Length in Centimeters

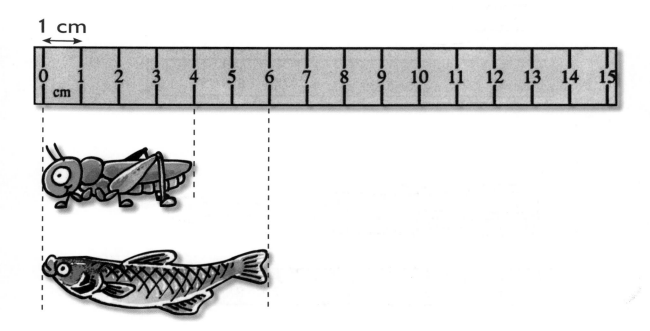

The **centimeter** is another unit of length.
We write **cm** for centimeters.
100 cm = 1 m

The grasshopper is 4 cm long.

The fish is 6 cm long.

The grasshopper is ▢ cm shorter than the fish.

The fish is ▢ cm longer than the grasshopper.

1. How many centimeters long are these things?

(a)

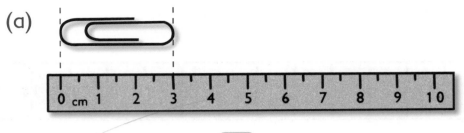

The paper clip is [ ] cm long.

(b)

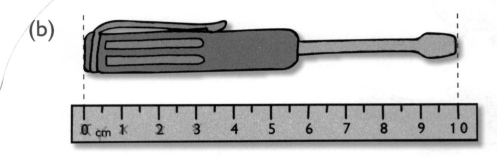

The screwdriver is [ ] cm long.

2. Use your ruler to measure the length and width of your textbook.

The length is about [ ] cm.

The width is about [ ] cm.

3. (a) Measure the length of your hand and your handspan in centimeters.

My hand is about

 cm long.

My handspan is about

 cm long.

(b) Which is longer, your hand or your handspan?
(c) How much longer?

Exercise 2, pages 73-75

4. Estimate and then measure the following lengths.

	My estimate	My measure
Length of my textbook	about ☐ cm	about ☐ cm
Length of my pencil	about ☐ cm	about ☐ cm
Length of my foot	about ☐ cm	about ☐ cm
Length of a drinking straw	about ☐ cm	about ☐ cm

5. Cut a piece of string as long as the line below.
   Then measure the length of the string with your ruler.

6. Measure these lines.

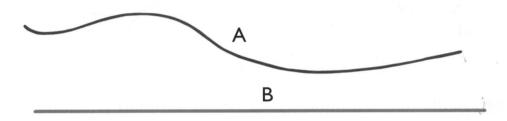

(a) Line A is about ▢ cm long.

(b) Line B is about ▢ cm long.

(c) Which line is longer?
(d) How much longer?

7. Susan is going to the post office.
   (a) Which is the shortest way?
   (b) Which is the longest way?

8. Use a measuring tape to measure your waist
    in centimeters.

Measuring tape

The length of my waist is about [ ] cm.

9. Work in groups.
    Use a measuring tape to measure your waist.
    Then measure the waists of three friends.
    Make a table to show your results.

Name	Length of waist
	about [ ] cm
	about [ ] cm
	about [ ] cm
	about [ ] cm

Exercise 3, pages 76-77

4 Measuring Length in Yards and Feet

We also measure length in yards and feet.

1. Measure your teacher's desk with a yard stick.

Is the length more than a yard?
Is the width more than a yard?

2. Measure your height with the yard stick.
Are you taller than 1 yard or shorter than 1 yard?

The **yard** is a unit of length.
We write **yd** for yard.

3. Cut a string 1 foot long.
   Use it to measure the length of your desk.

   Is the length of your desk more than 1 foot or less than 1 foot?

   The **foot** is a unit of length.
   If we have more than one foot, we call them feet.
   We write **ft** for foot or feet.

   We read 1 ft as 1 foot, and 2 ft as 2 feet.

4. Cut a string 1 foot long. Cut a string 1 yard long.
   Place the two strings side by side.

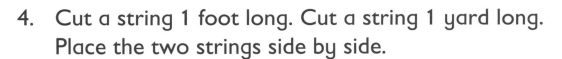

   String A ▭ 1 foot

   String B ▭ 1 yard

   Which string is longer?

   Cut several strings, each 1 foot long.
   How many 1-foot strings do you need to match the length of the 1-yard string?

   1 yard = ▢ **feet**

71

5 Measuring Length in Inches

We also measure length in inches.

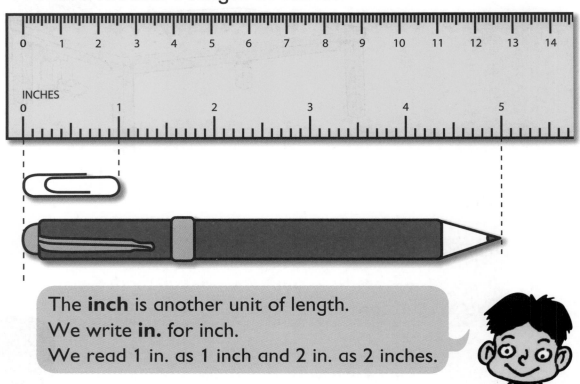

The **inch** is another unit of length.
We write **in.** for inch.
We read 1 in. as 1 inch and 2 in. as 2 inches.

The paper clip is 1 in. long.
The pen is 5 in. long.

The paper clip is ☐ in. shorter than the pen.

The pen is ☐ in. longer than the paper clip.

1 foot = 12 inches

1. Use your ruler to measure the length and width of your textbook.

    (a) The length is about ☐ in.

    (b) The width is about ☐ in.

2. (a) Compare yards with meters.

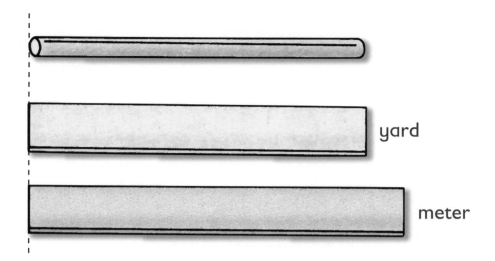

yard

meter

The rod is 1 yd long.
It is about 1 m long.

1 yard is just a little shorter than 1 meter.

(b) Compare inches with centimeters.

Line A <u>1 cm</u>

Line B <u>_____ 1 in. _____</u>

Which line is longer?

1 inch is longer than 1 centimeter.

We use feet, yards and meters to measure longer objects.
We use inches and centimeters to measure shorter objects.

Exercise 4, page 78

Find the value of each of the following:

	(a)	(b)	(c)
1.	285 + 9	329 + 70	454 + 46
2.	262 + 309	374 + 128	675 + 285
3.	392 − 8	267 − 80	473 − 95
4.	337 − 208	370 − 192	503 − 184
5.	624 + 176	400 − 196	800 − 106

6. These are regular patterns of numbers.
   What are the missing numbers?

   (a) 2, 4, 6, 8, ☐, ☐, ☐, 16, 20

   (b) 500, 490, 480, ☐, ☐, ☐, 440, ☐, 420

7.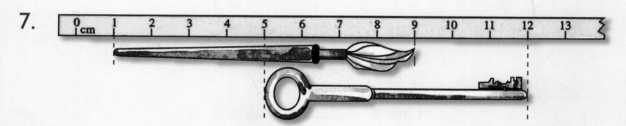

(a) Which is longer, the paintbrush or the key?

(b) The total length of the paintbrush and the key is ☐ cm.

(c) The total length of 2 similar keys is ☐ cm.

8. A bridge is 6 yd long.
   (a) Is it more than, less than or
       the same as 6 ft long?
   (b) Is it more than, less than or
       the same as 6 m long?

9. (a) What number is 10 more than 203?
   (b) What number is 100 more than 349?
   (c) What number is 1 less than 800?
   (d) What number is 100 less than 425?

10.

Shawn's house

550 m

350 m

Shawn walked from his house to the post office and then to the library.
How far did he walk?

11. Lily bought a ribbon 90 cm long.
    She had 35 cm of it left after making a bow.
    How many centimeters of ribbon did she use to make the bow?

12. What is the total length around the field?

24 yd

16 yd   Field   12 yd

12 yd

13. Taylor is 96 cm tall.
    Nicole is 8 cm shorter than Taylor.
    (a) What is Nicole's height?
    (b) What is their total height?

Review 3, pages 79-82

4 WEIGHT

1 Measuring Weight in Kilograms

The **kilogram** is a unit of weight.
We write **kg** for kilogram.

Hold a 1-kilogram weight
in your hand.
Feel how heavy it is.

The book weighs less than 1 kg.

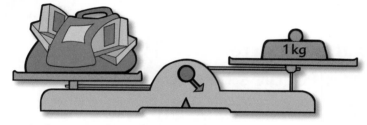

The bag weighs more than 1 kg.
Look for an object which weighs about 1 kg.

76

1. Make a bag of beans which weighs 1 kg.

2. (a)

The prawns weigh ⬜ kg.

(b)

The newspapers weigh ⬜ kg.

3.

Is the papaya heavier than 1 kg or lighter than 1 kg?

4.

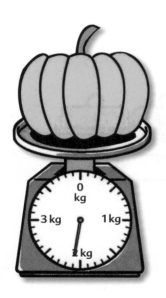

Is the weight of the pumpkin more than 2 kg or less than 2 kg?

5. The weight of the bag is kg.

6.

(a) Which package is heavier?

(b) How much heavier?

(c) What is the total weight of the two packages?

7.

(a) Which package is the heaviest?

(b) Which package is the lightest?

(c) What is the total weight of the three packages?

8. Work in groups.
   Get an object which you think weighs about 1 kg.
   Check the weight of the object with a weighing scale.
   Does it weigh more or less than 1 kg?

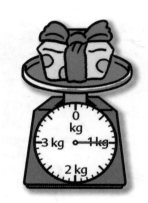

9. You need a weighing scale.
   Put a check (✓) in the correct box.

	less than 1 kg	more than 1 kg
Weight of a pair of shoes		
Weight of 5 textbooks		

10.

(a) Which fruit weighs more than 1 kg?

(b) Which fruit weighs 1 kg?

(c) Which fruit weighs less than 1 kg?

Exercise 1, page 83

2 Measuring Weight in Grams

The **gram** is another unit of weight.
We write **g** for gram.
1000 g = 1 kg

Find some of these objects and feel how heavy they are.

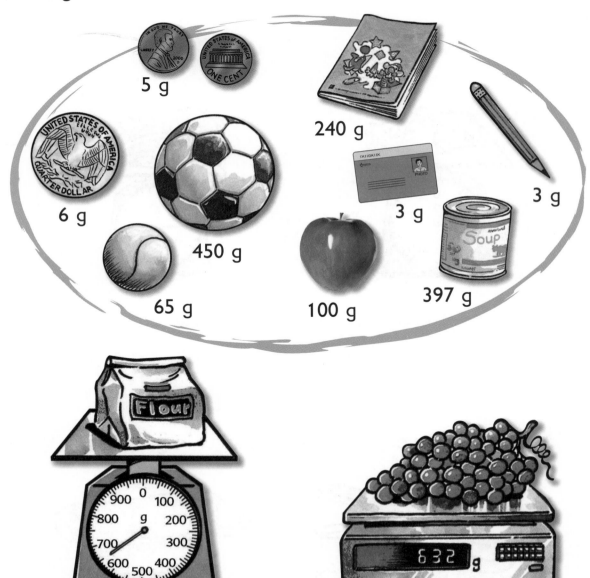

5 g

240 g

6 g

450 g

3 g

3 g

65 g

100 g

397 g

The flour weighs 650 g.

The grapes weigh 632 g.

1. (a)

The carrots weigh

 g.

(b)

The fish weighs

 g.

2. (a)

The mushrooms

weigh g.

(b)

The salad leaves

weigh g.

3. Measure the weight of these objects in grams.

a pair of scissors

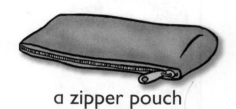

a zipper pouch

4. Work in groups.
    Estimate the weight of each of the following.
    Then check your guesses with a weighing scale.

	My estimate	My measure
a pencil	about ☐ g	about ☐ g
a mug	about ☐ g	about ☐ g
10 marbles	about ☐ g	about ☐ g

5.

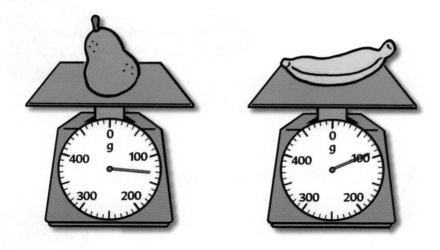

(a) The pear weighs ☐ g.

(b) The banana weighs ☐ g.

(c) The total weight of the fruit is ☐ g.

(d) The pear weighs ☐ g more than the banana.

Exercise 2, page 84

3 Measuring Weight in Pounds and Ounces

We also measure weight in pounds.

The **pound** is a unit of weight. We write **lb** for pound.

Hold a 1-pound weight in your hand. Feel how heavy it is.

1. Make a bag of beans which weighs 1 lb.

2.

Is the watermelon heavier than 1 lb or lighter than 1 lb?

3.

(a) Which package is lighter?

(b) How much lighter?

(c) Find the total weight of the two packages.

4. Find out your weight in pounds using a bathroom scale.

5. We also measure weight in ounces.

The **ounce** is another unit of weight.
We write **oz** for ounce.
16 oz = 1 lb

The apple weighs
[ ] oz.

The mushrooms weigh
[ ] oz.

6. Find the weight of these objects using a kitchen scale.

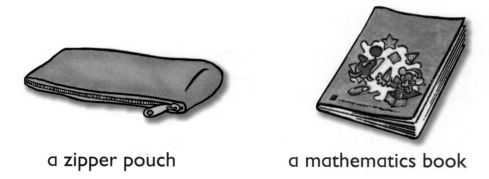

a zipper pouch

a mathematics book

7. Use a balance scale to help you.

(a) Compare pounds with kilograms.

Which is lighter?

1 pound is lighter than 1 kilogram.

(b) Compare ounces with grams.

Which is heavier?

1 ounce is heavier than 1 gram.

Exercise 3, pages 85-86

Find the value of each of the following:

	(a)	(b)	(c)
1.	253 + 8	368 + 40	476 + 57
2.	509 + 128	670 + 186	764 + 166
3.	202 − 9	357 − 70	402 − 82
4.	532 − 500	642 − 162	830 − 244
5.	843 − 289	267 + 356	804 − 269

6. (a)

The watermelon

weighs ☐ kg.

(b)

The vegetables

weigh ☐ g.

7. Write **>**, **<** or **=** in place of each .

(a) 1 kg ◯ 1 g   (b) 1 lb ◯ 1 kg

(c) 3 cm ◯ 3 m   (d) 12 ft ◯ 12 ft

(e) 10 oz ◯ 10 lb   (f) 6 in. ◯ 6 cm

(g) 12 in. ◯ 1 ft   (h) 32 ft ◯ 32 yd

(i) 20 oz ◯ 20 g   (j) 100 in. ◯ 100 ft

8. Find the missing numbers.

(a) $70 + \boxed{} = 78$ (b) $200 + \boxed{} = 208$

(c) $400 + \boxed{} = 490$ (d) $400 + \boxed{} = 409$

(e) $578 - \boxed{} = 508$ (f) $695 - \boxed{} = 690$

(g) $794 - \boxed{} = 694$ (h) $999 - \boxed{} = 949$

9. A lobster weighs 900 g.
   A crab weighs 550 g.
   (a) Which is heavier, the lobster or the crab?
   (b) How much heavier?

10. Raj weighs 39 kg.
    His father is 28 kg heavier than he.
    (a) Find the weight of Raj's father.
    (b) What is their total weight?

11. A pear weighs 280 g.
    An apricot is 60 g lighter than the pear.
    (a) What is the weight of the apricot?
    (b) Find the total weight of the pear and the apricot.

12. The total weight of an apple and a pineapple is 840 g.
    The apple weighs 90 g.
    (a) Find the weight of the pineapple.
    (b) How much heavier is the pineapple than the apple?

Review 4, pages 87-91

MULTIPLICATION AND DIVISION

1 Multiplication

How many apples are there altogether?

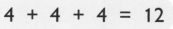

4 + 4 + 4 = 12

3 groups of 4

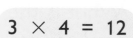

3 × 4 = 12

4 × 3 = 12

There are  apples altogether.

This is **multiplication**.
We multiply to find the total number.

1.

5×4

There are 5 birds in each nest.

There are birds in 4 nests.

2.

There are 5 groups of 6.

There are hats altogether.

5×6

Exercise 1, pages 92-93

3. (a) Multiply 7 by 3.

$7 \times 3 =$

(b) Multiply 9 by 4.

$9 \times 4 =$

Exercise 2, pages 94-95

4. (a)

$4 \times 2 =$

$2 \times 4 =$

(b)

$5 \times 3 =$

$3 \times 5 =$

92

Exercise 3, pages 96-97

1.

How many butterflies are there altogether?

2.

There are 2 buttons on each shirt.
How many buttons are there on 5 shirts?

3. There are 6 chairs in each row.
How many chairs are there
in 3 rows?

4. Jessica bought 3 boxes of cakes.
There were 5 cakes in each box.
How many cakes did she
buy altogether?

93

Exercise 4, pages 98-99

2 Division

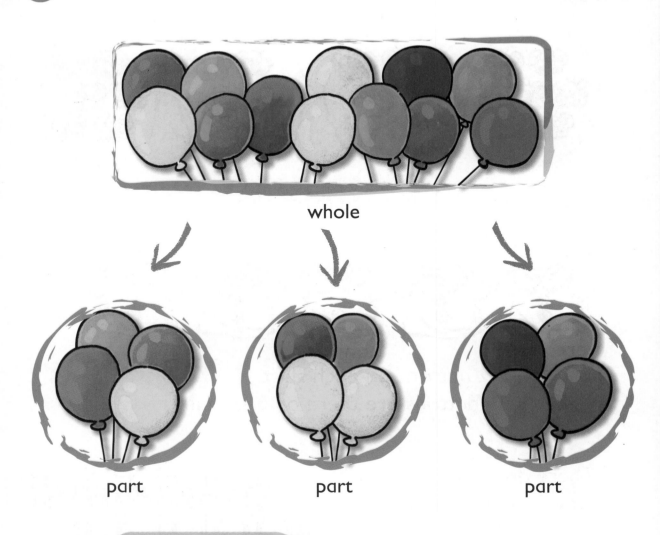

whole

part   part   part

Divide 12 balloons into groups of 4.

Divide 12 balloons into 3 equal groups.

1.

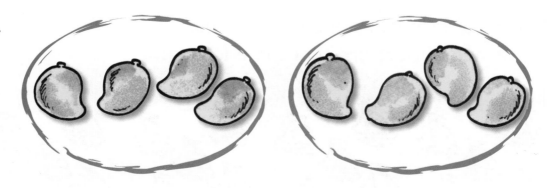

Divide 8 mangoes into 2 equal groups.
There are 4 mangoes in each group.

We write:

$$8 \div 2 = 4$$

Divide 8 by 2.
The answer is 4.

This is **division**.
We divide to find the
number in each group.

95

2. Divide 20 boats into 4 equal groups.
   How many boats are there in each group?

   20 ÷ 4 = ☐

   There are ☐ boats in each group.

3. Share 18 toy cars equally among 3 children.
   How many toy cars does each child get?

   18 ÷ 3 = ☐

   Each child gets ☐ toy cars.

4.

Divide 15 children into groups of 5.
There are 3 groups.

We write:

$$15 \div 5 = 3$$

Divide 15 by 5.
The answer is 3.

We also divide to find
the number of groups.

Exercise 5, pages 100-102

5. Divide 30 shells into groups of 6.
    How many groups are there?

    30 ÷ 6 = ☐

There are ☐ groups.

6. Lily uses 4 straws to make one square.
    How many squares can she make with 24 straws?

    24 ÷ 4 = ☐

She can make ☐ squares.

Exercise 6, pages 103-105

7.

$9 \times 2 = $ ☐ $2 \times 9 = $ ☐

$18 \div 2 = $ ☐ $18 \div 9 = $ ☐

8.

$8 \times 4 = $ ☐ $4 \times 8 = $ ☐

$32 \div 4 = $ ☐ $32 \div 8 = $ ☐

Exercise 7, pages 106-108

1. Share 12 oranges equally among 2 children.
   How many oranges does each child get?

2. Pack 24 balls into boxes of 6.
   How many boxes are there?

3. Emma tied 30 sticks into 3 equal bundles.
   How many sticks were there in each bundle?

4. Lauren makes 28 cakes.
   She wants to put 4 cakes in each box.
   How many boxes does she need?

Exercise 8, pages 109-110

Find the value of each of the following:

	(a)	(b)	(c)
1.	569 + 90	670 + 45	792 + 58
2.	327 + 650	296 + 364	465 + 535
3.	488 – 86	846 – 64	903 – 93
4.	743 – 243	622 – 272	520 – 488
5.	362 – 178	469 + 156	700 – 302

6. Samy bought 20 yd of rope.
   He used 7 yd of it to make a swing.
   How much rope was left?

7. Nicole used 96 cm of ribbon to tie a package.
   She used 85 cm of ribbon to tie another package.
   How many centimeters of ribbon did she use altogether?

8. The total weight of a pumpkin and
   a pear is 340 g.
   The pear weighs 95 g.
   What is the weight of the pumpkin?

9. Jordan bought 23 books and 17 posters at a bookshop.
   How many fewer posters than books did he buy?

10. Sulin weighs 34 kg.
    Her brother is 8 kg lighter than she.
    (a) What is the weight of her brother?
    (b) What is their total weight?

11. Write **>**, **<** or **=** in place of each .

    (a) 80 + 100 ⬤ 160

    (b) 340 + 610 ⬤ 950

    (c) 429 + 236 ⬤ 630

    (d) 150 + 765 ⬤ 900 + 25

    (e) 214 + 380 ⬤ 450 + 134

12.

    $7 \times 3 = $ ▢ $3 \times 7 = $ ▢

    $21 \div 3 = $ ▢ $21 \div 7 = $ ▢

13.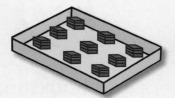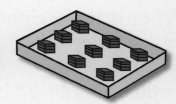

    Stacy baked 3 trays of brownies for a school trip.
    There were 9 brownies in each tray.
    How many brownies were there altogether?

14.

Mrs. Reed bought **18** pears.
She put **6** pears in each plastic bag.
How many bags of pears were there?

15.

Jake bought **5** bundles of books.
There were **4** books in each bundle.
How many books did he buy altogether?

16.

5 children share **35** cookies equally.
How many cookies does each child get?

MULTIPLICATION TABLES OF 2 AND 3

6

1 Multiplication Table of 2

Count the children by 2's.

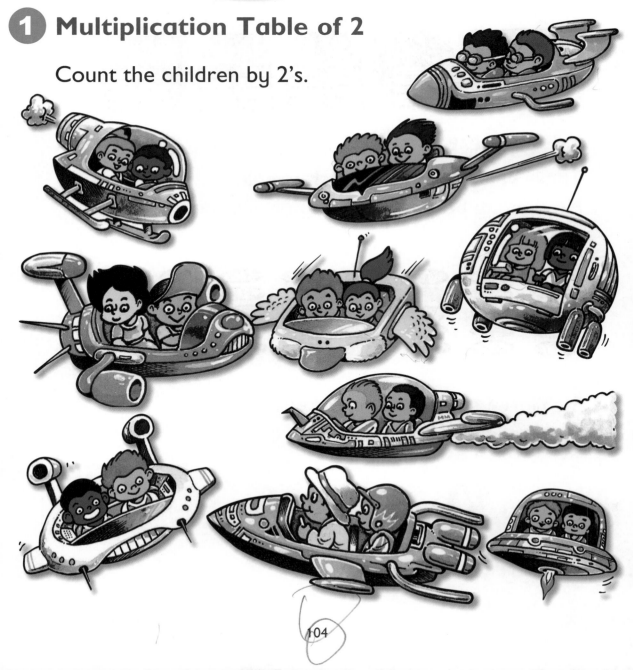

There are 2 children in each spaceship.
(a) How many children are there in 3 spaceships?

2 × 3 =

Count by 2's:
2, 4, 6

There are ⬚ children in 3 spaceships.

(b) How many children are there in 7 spaceships?

2 × 7 =

Count by 2's:
2, 4, 6, 8, 10, 12, 14

There are ⬚ children in 7 spaceships.

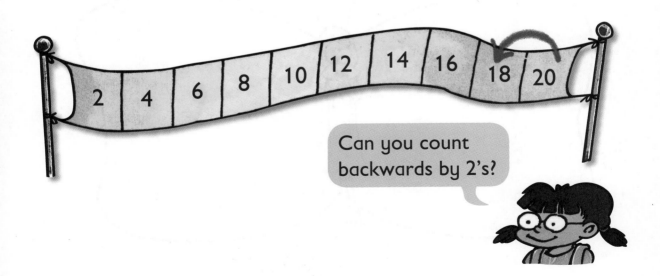

Can you count backwards by 2's?

105

1. (a) Multiply 2 by 2.

Count by 2's.

$2 \times 2 = $ ☐

(b) Multiply 2 by 9.

$2 \times 9 = $ ☐

Exercises 1 and 2, pages 115-120

2. Complete the number sentences.

$2 \times 1 = 2$

$2 \times 2 = 4$

$2 \times 3 = 6$

$2 \times 4 = $ ☐

$2 \times 5 = $ ☐

$2 \times 6 = $ ☐

$2 \times 7 = $ ☐

$2 \times 8 = $ ☐

$2 \times 9 = $ ☐

$2 \times 10 = $ ☐

3. (a) Multiply 2 by 3.

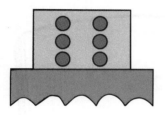

$2 \times 3 = $ ☐

(b) Multiply 2 by 4.

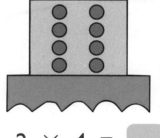

$2 \times 4 = $ ☐

4.

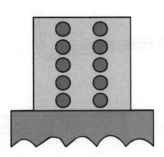

$2 \times 5 = 10$

$2 \times 6 = $ ☐

2 more

Exercise 3, pages 121-122

5. (a)

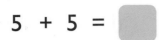

$5 + 5 = $ ☐

$5 \times 2 = $ ☐

(b)

$7 + 7 = $ ☐

$7 \times 2 = $ ☐

6. (a) $8 + 8 = $ ☐

$8 \times 2 = $ ☐

(b) $9 + 9 = $ ☐

$9 \times 2 = $ ☐

7. Complete the number sentences.

1 × 2 = 2

2 × 2 = 4

3 × 2 = 6

4 × 2 =

5 × 2 =

6 × 2 =

7 × 2 =

8 × 2 =

9 × 2 =

10 × 2 =

8. What are the missing numbers?

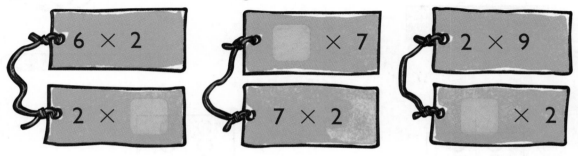

6 × 2

2 ×

× 7

7 × 2

2 × 9

× 2

Exercise 4, pages 123-124

9. Find the value of
(a) 2 × 3
(b) 4 × 2
(c) 2 × 2
(d) 1 × 2
(e) 9 × 2
(f) 2 × 8
(g) 2 × 6
(h) 7 × 2
(i) 2 × 10
(j) 5 × 2
(k) 3 × 2
(l) 2 × 4
(m) 2 × 9
(n) 6 × 2
(o) 2 × 7

10. True or false?
(a) 2 × 3 = 2 × 3
(b) 2 × 5 = 2 + 3
(c) 6 × 2 = 5 + 2
(d) 8 + 8 = 2 × 8
(e) 2 × 2 = 2 + 2
(f) 2 × 10 = 5 + 5

Exercise 5, pages 125-127

11. Meihua bought 6 strings.
Each string was 2 m long.
What was the total length of the strings?

2 m

$6 \times 2 = \boxed{}$

The total length was $\boxed{}$ m.

12. A bird has 2 wings.
How many wings do 6 birds have?

13. At a party, each child gets 2 balloons.
How many balloons do 10 children get?

14. Ian saves $5 a week.
How much can he save in 2 weeks?

15. Lauren bought 4 bags of ground coffee.
Each bag weighed 2 kg.
How many kilograms of ground coffee did she buy?

16. Morgan made 2 sets of curtains.
She used 8 m of cloth for each
set of curtains.
How many meters of cloth
did she use altogether?

Exercise 6, pages 128-129

2 Multiplication Table of 3

Count the cars by 3's.

There are 3 cars in each row.

(a) How many cars are there in 5 rows?

$3 \times 5 =$

Count by 3's:
3, 6, 9, 12, 15

There are cars in 5 rows.

(b) How many cars are there in 9 rows?

$3 \times 9 =$

Count by 3's:
3, 6, 9, 12, 15,
18, 21, 24, 27

There are cars in 9 rows.

1. (a) Multiply 3 by 4.

$3 \times 4 =$

Count by 3's.

(b) Multiply 3 by 8.

$3 \times 8 =$

Exercise 7, pages 130-134

2.

$3 \times 6 =$ ☐

$6 \times 3 =$ ☐

3. What are the missing numbers?

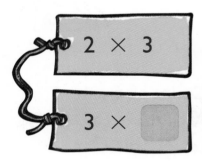

2×3
$3 \times$ ☐

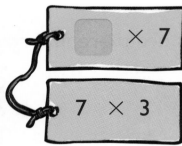

☐ $\times 7$
7×3

3×8
☐ $\times 3$

4. Complete the number sentences.

 Exercise 8, pages 135-136

$3 \times 1 = 3$ $1 \times 3 =$ ☐

$3 \times 2 = 6$ $2 \times 3 =$ ☐

$3 \times 3 = 9$ $3 \times 3 =$ ☐

$3 \times 4 =$ ☐ $4 \times 3 =$ ☐

$3 \times 5 =$ ☐ $5 \times 3 =$ ☐

$3 \times 6 =$ ☐ $6 \times 3 =$ ☐

$3 \times 7 =$ ☐ $7 \times 3 =$ ☐

$3 \times 8 =$ ☐ $8 \times 3 =$ ☐

$3 \times 9 =$ ☐ $9 \times 3 =$ ☐

$3 \times 10 =$ ☐ $10 \times 3 =$ ☐

5.

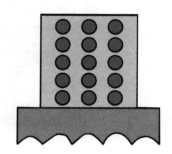

$$3 \times 5 = 15$$

$$3 \times 6 = \boxed{}$$

6. $3 \times 10 = 30$

$3 \times 9 = 27$

$3 \times 8 = \boxed{}$

Exercise 9, pages 137-140

7. Find the value of
    (a) 3×1 (b) 2×3 (c) 3×4
    (d) 6×3 (e) 7×3 (f) 3×8
    (g) 4×3 (h) 5×3 (i) 3×10
    (j) 3×7 (k) 9×3 (l) 3×3
    (m) 8×3 (n) 10×3 (o) 3×6

8. True or false?
    (a) $3 \times 2 = 3 + 3$ (b) $3 \times 3 = 3 + 3 + 3$
    (c) $3 \times 6 = 15 + 6$ (d) $3 \times 9 = 30 - 3$
    (e) $3 \times 8 = 8 \times 3$ (f) $3 \times 10 = 2 \times 10$

Exercise 10, pages 141-142

9. Sumin bought 7 bags of sugar.
    Each bag weighed 3 kg.
    How many kilograms of sugar did he
    buy altogether?

$$7 \times 3 = \boxed{}$$

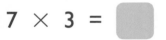

He bought ☐ kg of sugar.

10. There are 3 wheels on a tricycle.
    How many wheels are there on 4 tricycles?

11. There are 7 trees in one row.
    How many trees are there in 3 rows?

12. One bag of potatoes weighs 8 kg.
    What is the weight of 3 bags of potatoes?

13. Michelle made 6 dresses.
    She used 3 yd of cloth for each dress.
    How many yards of cloth did she use altogether?

14. Matthew bought 3 sets of stamps.
    There were 10 stamps in each set.
    How many stamps did he buy?

Exercise 11, pages 143-144

Find the value of each of the following:

	(a)	(b)	(c)
1.	2 × 1	1 × 3	4 × 2
2.	2 × 5	4 × 3	2 × 9
3.	8 × 2	3 × 9	3 × 3
4.	10 × 2	8 × 3	3 × 7
5.	2 × 7	3 × 5	6 × 3

6. Nicole can read 3 storybooks a week.
    How many storybooks can she read in 5 weeks?

7. One concert ticket costs $7.
    Mr. Garcia buys 2 tickets.
    How much does he pay?

8. A bee has 6 legs.
    How many legs do 3 bees have?

9. Mrs. Moore made 9 pillow cases.
    She used 2 m of lace for each pillow case.
    How many meters of lace did she use altogether?

10. Stephanie bought 3 bags of rice flour.
    Each bag weighed 10 lb.
    How many pounds of rice flour did she buy?

Exercise 12, pages 145-147

3 Dividing by 2

Put 6 flowers equally into 2 vases.

$$3 \times 2 = 6$$

$6 \div 2 =$

Put 10 flowers equally into 2 vases.

$$5 \times 2 = 10$$

$10 \div 2 =$

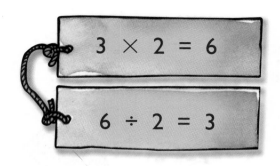

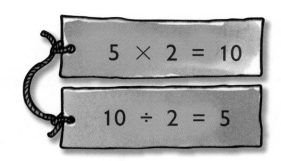

1. (a)

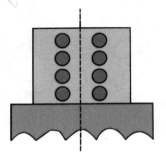

$4 \times 2 = 8$

$8 \div 2 = \boxed{}$

(b)

$7 \times 2 = 14$

$14 \div 2 = \boxed{}$

2. What are the missing numbers?

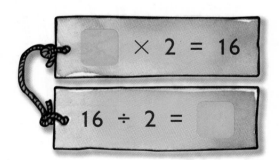

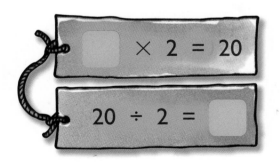

Exercise 13, pages 148-149

3. Meili has **8** flowers.
   She puts them equally into **2** vases.
   How many flowers are there in each vase?

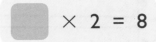 × 2 = 8

8 ÷ 2 =

There are flowers in each vase.

4. Danielle has 14 flowers.
   She wants to put **2** flowers in each vase.
   How many vases does she need?

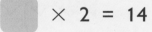 × 2 = 14

14 ÷ 2 =

She needs vases.

5. Kristin has a string 12 m long.
   She cuts it into equal pieces.
   Each piece is 2 m long.
   How many pieces of string does she get?

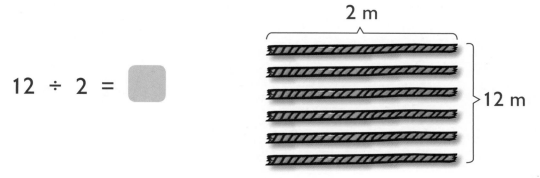

$12 \div 2 =$ ☐

She gets ☐ pieces of string.

6. Justin has a string 18 m long.
   He cuts it into 2 equal pieces.
   How long is each piece?

$18 \div 2 =$ ☐

Each piece is ☐ m long.

Find the value of each of the following:

	(a)	(b)	(c)
1.	4 × 2	5 × 2	2 × 2
2.	8 ÷ 2	10 ÷ 2	4 ÷ 2
3.	6 × 2	9 × 2	8 × 2
4.	12 ÷ 2	18 ÷ 2	16 ÷ 2
5.	14 ÷ 2	2 ÷ 2	20 ÷ 2

6. Nathan arranged 20 chairs in 2 rows.
   He put the same number of chairs in each row.
   How many chairs were there in each row?

7. Dakota saved $2 a day.
   How many days did she take to save $18?

8. Mrs. Ricci bought 2 kg of grapes.
   1 kg of grapes cost $5.
   How much did she pay for the grapes?

9. Kevin had a rope 16 m long.
   He cut it into 2 equal pieces.
   Find the length of each piece.

10. Nicole makes 14 pies.
    She wants to put 2 pies each in a box.
    How many boxes does she need?

Exercise 14, pages 150-151

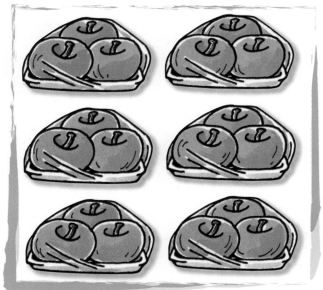

Divide 18 apples into groups of 3.

There are groups.

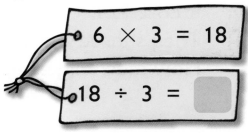

$6 \times 3 = 18$

$18 \div 3 = \boxed{}$

1. **What are the missing numbers?**

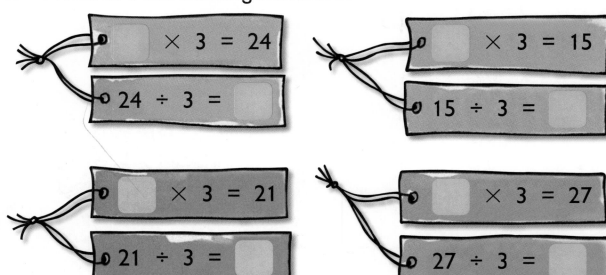

$\boxed{} \times 3 = 24$

$24 \div 3 = \boxed{}$

$\boxed{} \times 3 = 15$

$15 \div 3 = \boxed{}$

$\boxed{} \times 3 = 21$

$21 \div 3 = \boxed{}$

$\boxed{} \times 3 = 27$

$27 \div 3 = \boxed{}$

Exercise 15, pages 152-153

2. Mr. Wang bought 30 apples at 3 for $1.
   How much did he pay?

$$30 \div 3 = \boxed{10}$$

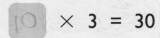

$$\boxed{10} \times 3 = 30$$

He paid $ \boxed{10} .

3. 3 children bought a present for their friend.
   It cost $24.
   They shared the cost equally.
   How much did each child pay?

$$24 \div 3 = \boxed{8}$$

$$\boxed{8} \times 3 = 24$$

Each child paid $ \boxed{8} .

Find the value of each of the following:

	(a)	(b)	(c)
1.	4 × 3	6 × 3	5 × 3
2.	12 ÷ 3	18 ÷ 3	15 ÷ 3
3.	9 × 3	7 × 3	8 × 3
4.	27 ÷ 3	21 ÷ 3	24 ÷ 3
5.	9 ÷ 3	6 ÷ 3	30 ÷ 3

6. Ricardo packed 30 bottles equally into 3 boxes.
   How many bottles were there in each box?

7. Devi paid $18 for 3 kg of cherries.
   Find the cost of 1 kg of cherries.

8. David had 15 toy soldiers.
   He lined them up in 3 rows.
   There were the same number of soldiers in each row.
   How many toy soldiers were there in each row?

9. Matthew bought 9 books.
   Each book cost $3.
   How much did he pay altogether?

10. There are 24 beads on 3 strings.
    There are the same number of beads on each string.
    How many beads are there on each string?

Exercise 16, pages 154-155

PRACTICE D

Find the value of each of the following:

	(a)	(b)	(c)
1.	10 ÷ 2	14 ÷ 2	8 ÷ 2
2.	9 ÷ 3	15 ÷ 3	12 ÷ 3
3.	12 ÷ 2	16 ÷ 2	20 ÷ 2
4.	18 ÷ 3	24 ÷ 3	21 ÷ 3
5.	18 ÷ 2	30 ÷ 3	27 ÷ 3

6. Emily had a ribbon 24 cm long.
   She cut it into 3 equal pieces.
   Find the length of each piece.

7. Sam saved $3 a week.
   How many weeks did he take to save $30?

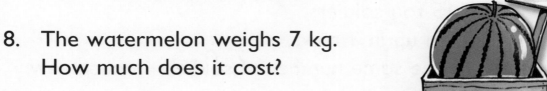

8. The watermelon weighs 7 kg.
   How much does it cost?

9. A shopkeeper packed 16 kg of flour into bags.
   Each bag weighed 2 kg.
   How many bags did he get?

10. Mr. Chen bought 18 pears.
    How much did he pay?

Exercises 17 to 19, pages 156-162

Find the value of each of the following:

	(a)	(b)	(c)
1.	400 + 8	500 + 90	375 + 180
2.	678 − 600	798 − 95	920 − 186
3.	2 × 9	3 × 8	8 × 2
4.	18 ÷ 2	24 ÷ 3	16 ÷ 2
5.	21 ÷ 3	20 ÷ 2	30 ÷ 3

6. Write >, < or = in place of each ⬤.

(a) 309 ⬤ 390

(b) 410 ⬤ 408

(c) 18 + 8 ⬤ 16 + 7

(d) 850 + 103 ⬤ 13 + 940

7.

(a) The pear weighs ⬜ g.

(b) The apple weighs ⬜ g.

8. The total length of three sides of this triangle is 30 in. What is the length of the shortest side?

12 in. 10 in.

?

9. Complete these regular number patterns.

    (a) 123, 143, ☐, ☐, 203, ☐

    (b) 705, ☐, 505, 405, ☐, 205

    (c) ☐, 9, 12, ☐, 18, 21, ☐

10. Bonita bought some apples for $5.
    How many apples did she buy?

3 for $1

11. There are 128 boys.
    There are 25 more girls than boys.
    How many girls are there?

12. Mary is 142 cm tall.
    She is 14 cm taller than her brother.
    What is her brother's height?

13. Mrs. Goodman made 24 cream puffs for a party.
    She placed 3 cream puffs on each plate.
    How many plates did she use?

14.

    Mark used this ruler to measure the length of his pencil
    in both inches and centimeters.
    Which is greater, the number of inches or the
    number of centimeters?

15. The chart shows the number of
    members in a chess club.
    How many members are there
    in the chess club?

Men	: 128
Women	: 94
Children	: 46

16. Tasha wants to buy this violin.
    She has only $89.
    How much more money does
    she need?

$120

17. Mrs. Gray bought 3 boxes of cakes.
    There were 6 cakes in each box.
    How many cakes did she buy?

18. 3 children shared $27 equally.
    How much money did each child receive?

19. There are 820 palm trees.
    There are 95 more coconut trees than palm trees.
    How many coconut trees are there?

20. Jordan has $145.
    He needs $65 more to buy this camera.
    How much does the camera cost?

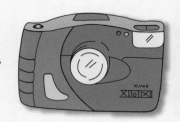

21. A tailor used 18 m of cloth to make shirts.
    He used 2 m of cloth for each shirt.
    How many shirts did he make?

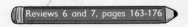

GLOSSARY

Word	Meaning
centimeter	The **centimeter** is a unit of length. We write '**cm**' for centimeter. 100 cm = 1 m  The pen is 10 cm long. 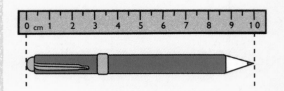
division	To put into equal groups. We **divide** to find the number in each group. Divide 12 cherries into 2 equal groups. There are 6 cherries in each group. 12 ÷ 2 = 6 We also **divide** to find the number of equal groups. Divide 12 cherries into groups of 6. There are 2 equal groups. 12 ÷ 6 = 2 We write '÷' to mean divide. 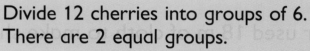

Word	Meaning
foot	The foot is a unit of length. We write '**ft**' for foot. $$3 \text{ ft} = 1 \text{ yd}$$ String A ▬ 1 **foot** String B ▬▬▬ 1 yard
gram	The **gram** is a unit of weight. We write '**g**' for gram. $$1000 \text{ g} = 1 \text{ kg}$$ The mushrooms weigh 350 g.
greater than	$$250 > 200$$ 250 is **greater than** 200. We write '>' to mean **greater than**.

Word	Meaning
hundreds	 	Hundreds	Tens	Ones
---	---	---
6	4	2	 642 = 6 **hundreds** 4 tens 2 ones
inch	The **inch** is a unit of length. We write '**in.**' for inch. 12 in. = 1 ft  The paper clip is 1 in. long.
kilogram	The **kilogram** is a unit of weight. We write '**kg**' for kilogram. 1 kg = 1000 g  The grapes weigh 1 kg.

Word	Meaning
less than	 200 < 250 200 is **less than** 250. We write '<' to mean **less than**.
meter	The **meter** is a unit of length. We write '**m**' for meter. $$1 \text{ m} = 100 \text{ cm}$$ *Example:* The boy is taller than 1 meter.
multiplication	To put together equal groups. 3 + 3 + 3 + 3 + 3 + 3 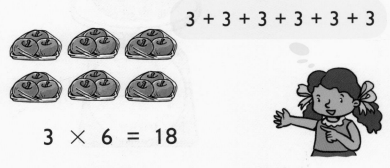 $$3 \times 6 = 18$$ We write '**X**' to mean multiply.

Word	Meaning
ounce	The **ounce** is a unit of weight. We write '**oz**' for ounce. 16 oz = 1 lb

The apple weighs 6 oz.

Word	Meaning
pound	The **pound** is a unit of weight. We write '**lb**' for pound. 1 lb = 16 oz

The watermelon weighs 6 lb.

Word	Meaning
renaming	We sometimes need to **rename** numbers when adding and subtracting.

When we rename numbers, we change:
- 10 ones to 1 ten or 1 ten to 10 ones;
- 10 tens to 1 hundred or 1 hundred to 10 tens;
- 10 hundreds to 1 thousand or 1 thousand to 10 hundreds.

For example,
in addition,

$$
\begin{array}{r}
^{1} \\
3\ 6 \\
+\ 2\ 8 \\
\hline
4
\end{array}
\qquad
\begin{array}{r}
^{1} \\
3\ 6 \\
+\ 2\ 8 \\
\hline
6\ 4
\end{array}
$$

Add the ones.   **Add the tens.**

in subtraction,

$$
\begin{array}{r}
^{5}\ \ ^{12} \\
\cancel{6}\ \cancel{2} \\
-\ 4\ 3 \\
\hline
9
\end{array}
\qquad
\begin{array}{r}
^{5}\ \ ^{12} \\
\cancel{6}\ \cancel{2} \\
-\ 4\ 3 \\
\hline
1\ 9
\end{array}
$$

Subtract the ones.   **Subtract the tens.**

Word	Meaning
yard	The **yard** is a unit of length. We write '**yd**' for yard. $1 \text{ yd} = 3 \text{ ft}$ String A ▬▬▬ 1 foot String B ▬▬▬▬▬▬▬ 1 **yard**

Index

addition
- addition problems with one- and two-digit numbers, *9, 12, 24-31, 33*
- addition problems with three-digit numbers, *32-34, 40-46, 56*
- addition with renaming, *39-45*
- addition without renaming, *32-34*
- meaning of, *24*

comparing numbers
- greater than, *20*
- less than, *20*
- small, smallest, *21*

count
- by 2's, *104-106*
- by 3's, *110-111*
- by hundreds, *13-18*
- by tens, *9-10*
- count backwards, *22, 105*
- count on, *22*

division
- by 2, *116-119*
- by 3, *121-122*
- division facts, *94*

grouping objects
- in hundreds, *13-19*
- in tens, *8-12*

length
- centimeters, *65-69*
- feet, *70-71*
- inches, *72-73*
- longer, longest, *65-68*
- meters, *61-64*
- shorter, shortest, *61, 68*
- taller, *61*
- yards, *70-71*

measurement
- length, *61-73*
- nonstandard units, *59-60*
- weight, *76-87*

multiplication
- multiplication facts, *90*
- table of 2, *104-108*
- table of 3, *110-113*

number bonds
- part, *24-26*
- whole, *24-26*

operational symbols
- division, *95, 97*
- multiplication, *91*

subtraction
- meaning of, *25*
- subtraction problems with one- and two-digit numbers, *25-31*
- subtraction problems with three-digit numbers, *35-38, 47-56*
- subtraction with renaming, *47-54*
- subtraction without renaming, *35-37*

weight
- grams, *81-83*
- heavier, heaviest, *79, 87*
- kilograms, *76-80*
- lighter, lightest, *78-79, 85, 87*
- ounces, *84-87*
- pounds, *84-87*

Blank